Table of Contents

INTRODUCTION 3

SECTION ONE 4

    What is LinkedIn 4

    What information can I get from LinkedIn 4

    LinkedIn Sales Navigator vs LinkedIn Premium 5

    How LinkedIn Sales Navigator Helps You Generate Leads
    10

    Finding Emails on LinkedIn 11

    InMail messages 12

SECTION TWO 13

USE THESE AND GET CONVERSIONS 13

    9 LinkedIn Prospecting Tips 13

    LinkedIn Lead Generation Proven Hack 18

    Post Daily Updates 19

    Join Groups 20

Try LinkedIn Premium 20

Benefits of LinkedIn Premium.. 21

Is LinkedIn Premium worth the investment?...................... 28

CONCLUSION... 30

INTRODUCTION

For nearly 2 decades now, LinkedIn has been professionals' definitive social media platform. If you are looking to connect with your coworkers, look for a job, or just expand your network, it is a platform unlike any other. But one of the best uses for LinkedIn is as a sales tool. If you know how to tap its full potential, you can use it to generate a steady stream of leads, learn more about your customers, and even begin the sales engagement process — especially in conjunction with a compatible sales engagement platform.

While it is possible to accomplish this using the free features of your LinkedIn account, it is probably better to upgrade with LinkedIn Sales Navigator.

So, what exactly is LinkedIn Sales Navigator, and how can you use it in your sales strategy? These and some other resounding queries are aptly addressed in this definitive guide. Isn't this for you?

SECTION ONE

What is LinkedIn

LinkedIn is a business social media platform. No matter if you are a sole trader, or own an international company like Apple, LinkedIn is for all. It allows professionals to connect, interact and even share posts about things that are interesting to them or even their industry.

The main bonus to LinkedIn is that you can control the people in your network. This is done via connections. Connecting to key decisions makers, businesses you want to work with, or even influential people within your industry allow you to really narrow your contacts down.

What information can I get from LinkedIn

Information is available in abundance on LinkedIn. Unlike most platforms people will have their email address, work and also location. Some even have direct contact numbers. Now taking advantage of this may seem like a great idea, however be warned. Sending sales pitches, and trying to sell without getting to know people can sometimes not go down to well. The best way to use this information is to make introductions. Introduce yourself, say hello, ask more about what they do and go from there.

Also, LinkedIn allows you to recommend people. When someone posts an update saying they are looking for something, you can tag people you know. This is a great way to introduce your services, and potentially find people who are looking for your services

LinkedIn Sales Navigator vs LinkedIn Premium

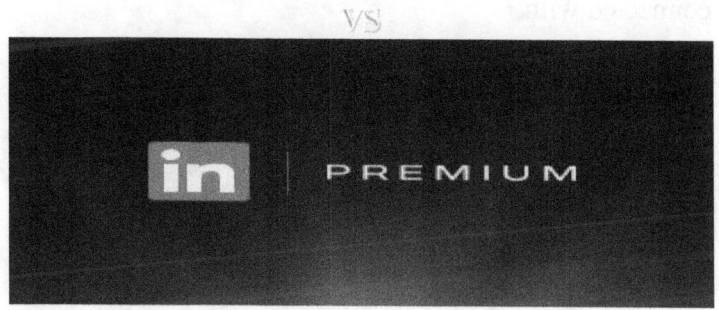

There are essentially two plans to choose from: Sales Navigator Professional and Sales Navigator Team.

Sales Navigator Professional is the core product, and is designed for individuals. Sales Navigator Team is basically the same thing, with a few extra features designed to help team members collaborate with each other. Your only deciding factor here is the number of team members you have.

With either, you will get:

20 InMail messages per month: InMail is a system that allows you to send a private message to another LinkedIn member, even if you are not connected. Ordinarily, you are restricted to sending messages only to people you have connected with.

LinkedIn Sales Navigator gives you 20 InMail messages per month, so you can reach out to prospects even if you are not connected with them. It is great for generating new leads.

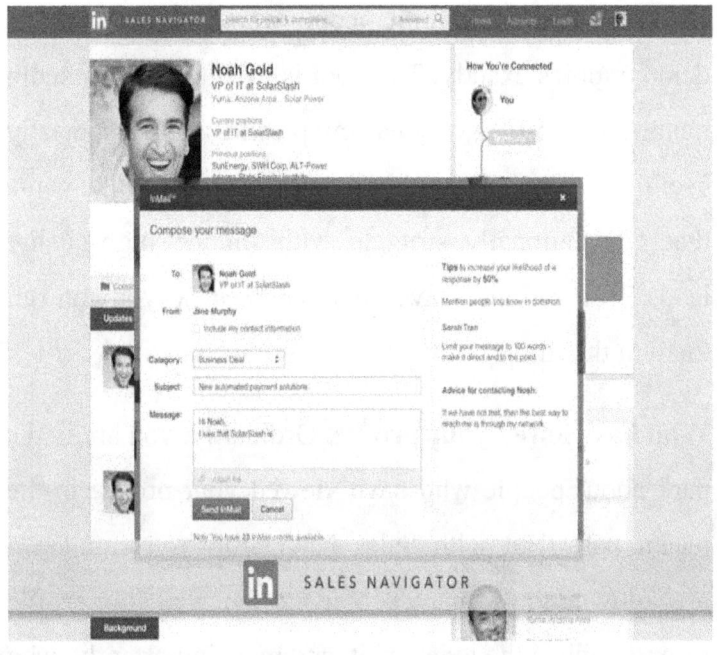

News and Insights: You will also get a built-in dashboard which allows you to get news and read insights related to potential leads in and near your network. For example, you can get notifications on recent job changes, announcements on company growth, and even new lead opportunities.

Advanced Search with Lead Builder: You will also have access to an *"Advanced Search"* function, which allows you to find specific people who match your target demographics exactly. This tool is used to find LinkedIn members who fit a very narrow profile, and is especially useful for companies and individual businesses like yours that conventionally struggle with finding high-quality leads. You can also save your searches, so you can run them in the future.

Who has viewed your profile. Ordinarily, you are in the dark about people who have viewed your profile in the recent past. But with Sales Navigator, you can get a breakdown of how many people have viewed your profile recently, when they viewed it, and most importantly, who they are. It is a good way to identify people who might be interested in you and your business.

Unlimited browsing (up to 3rd degree): Once you activate Sales Navigator, you will have unlimited access to browse profiles from search results up to 3rd degree connections. And as you will quickly discover, 3rd degree connections give you extensive coverage—especially if you make new 1st degree connections aggressively.

Lead recommendations: Running searches and discovering new leads based on your specified criteria is very helpful, but it is even better to get active lead recommendations. LinkedIn will monitor your search criteria and past outreach habits to recommend new leads to you and your team; you can follow up on these as you see fit.

Saved leads: You can also save leads for future interactions; and if you are relying on the team-based version of this tool, you can assign leads to others as well. There are also several minor features you will discover when you begin to explore this tool, meant to make your life easier and help you find more valuable leads.

As you might expect, you can sign up for a free trial. After a one-month trial use, the price allotted as according for individual. Team and Enterprise plans are also available, with the price scaling accordingly.

How LinkedIn Sales Navigator Helps You Generate Leads

LinkedIn Sales Navigator helps your lead generation and sales strategies in three main ways. As you will see, there are a variety of tools and features you can use for each of these main paths.

1. Target the right people

The most popular way to use Sales Navigator is as a way to generate leads by using advanced search to identify people in your target audience. Social media opens the door to billions of potential individuals, but effective lead generation is not about quantity; it is about quality. LinkedIn's advanced search and lead recommendation engines are perfect for narrowing your search to just the right people.

2. Understand your key demographics

You can also improve your conversion rates, your marketing strategy, and your close ratios by better understanding your key demographics. Again, Sales Navigator helps you do this. You will be able to get data on a wide range of individuals and businesses you might otherwise never encounter.

3. Engage with new prospects

Finally, you will get more opportunities to engage with new prospects. You can set up alerts so you can reach out to people at the right time, and with InMail, you can readily engage with people even if you do not have an immediate mutual connection in common.

Finding Emails on LinkedIn

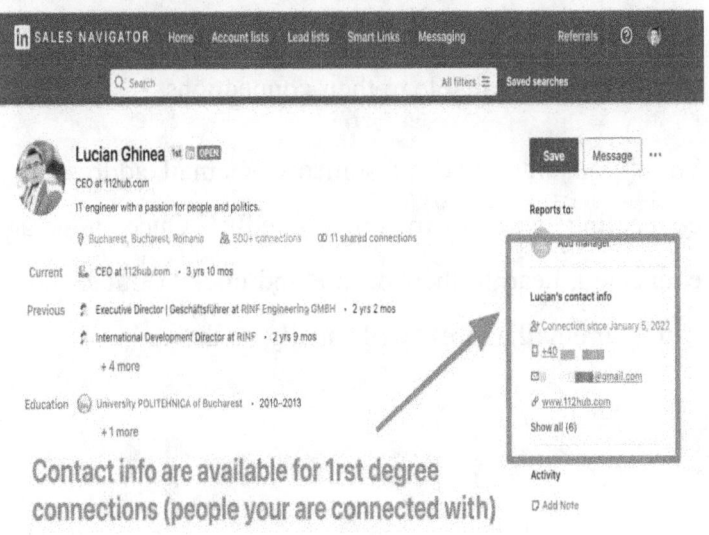

Remember that with LinkedIn Sales Navigator, you will have the ability to send InMail messages to 20 (or more, if you upgrade) people per month, regardless of how or if they are connected to you.

But what if you want to reach out to more? Or what if you want to send people an email, rather than a social media message? This is the gap InMail messages come to fill.

InMail messages

LinkedIn does not provide you with a direct way to get a user's email address. However, many people make their email address available to their connections.

So if you want to find someone's email address, try connecting with them on LinkedIn! Once you are connected, head to their profile and click "Contact info" and their email address will usually be there.

SECTION TWO
USE THESE AND GET CONVERSIONS

9 LinkedIn Prospecting Tips

LinkedIn Sales Navigator will enable more success in your sales team, but only if you are using it effectively. These tips can help you get the most out of this tool. Let us check them out together.

1. Use LinkedIn as one of many channels

LinkedIn is an amazing tool but it has limitations. Not every professional has a LinkedIn profile, and even if they do, they may make themselves hard to find, or may not have up-to-date information on their profiles. Accordingly, it is a good idea to use LinkedIn as one of several lead generation channels. Over time, you will be able to learn whether LinkedIn is average, or better or worse than average.

2. Make use of Saved Leads

When you are doing demographic research or are drumming up leads, you would not have time to reach out to everyone. That is why it is important to utilize the Saved Leads function, and save individuals and organizations to follow up with later.

3. Set alerts to trigger follow-ups

Alerts are only effective if you use them, so set them regularly to capitalize on them. You can set alerts whenever one of your leads takes a chosen meaningful action, like updating their job title or moving to a new company. Then, all you have to do is follow up in a timely manner.

4. Save your searches

After spending several minutes or longer defining the perfect search to find leads for your business, the last thing you will want to do is repeat the effort again in the future. Save time by saving all your searches, so you can repeat them easily later on.

5. Make use of Sales Spotlights

At the top of your screen, you will get a "Sales Spotlight" breakdown, which includes information you can use to narrow down your search. For example, you might see 200 people who have recently changed jobs, or 70 people who currently follow your company on the platform. Click on these spotlight items to see a breakdown of the profiles that belong to this category.

6. Reverse engineer lead searches

Instead of speculating on the demographic and profile bits of information that might make for a good lead, look at a current breakdown of your best customers. What do these people have in common? Which qualities would you like to see in leads and customers in the future? Use these data to reverse engineer new searches to perform in Sales Navigator in the future.

7. Optimize your team's LinkedIn profiles

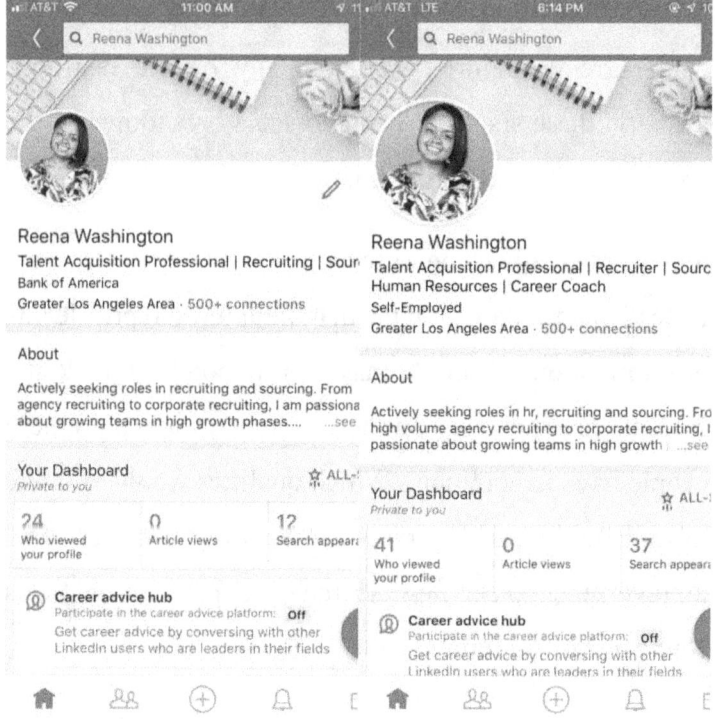

Remember, LinkedIn is not just about finding new people and reaching out to them. It is also about putting your best foot forward, and making your own profiles more visible to boost your reputation. Accordingly, it is important to optimize the LinkedIn profiles of your team as you start using LinkedIn Sales Navigator.

8. Use TeamLink

TeamLink is a tool that allows you to quickly and easily search within the connections and networks of your team members. It is a convenient way to find new leads that are just within reach—and once you identify them, you should have an opportunity to make a warm introduction via their closest connection.

9. Collaborate

Finally, while it is possible to use LinkedIn Sales Navigator as an individual almost exclusively, the true power of the platform is unlocked when you use it as a team. Use it to mutually exchange information, expand all your networks, and assign different leads to the people most capable of taking them. When all your sales representatives learn to think and act as a team, everyone will perform better—and you will get the best possible value out of Sales Navigator.

LinkedIn Lead Generation Proven Hack

Let me start by explaining the basic premise of LinkedIn Sales Navigator, and how it works for sales teams. First, you should be sure you want to upgrade to Sales Navigator rather than LinkedIn Premium. Anyways, the choice is yours at the end.

Using LinkedIn for Lead Generation can be done in a variety of ways. In actual fact, it is one of very few social media channels in which leads can be clear to see. Some of the ways in which you can find, and also generate leads follow next. I call them the Proven Hack and tag it PPJ.

Publish Articles

As with all marketing, content is going to be a great way to demonstrate your expertise in your chosen field. LinkedIn is no exception, in actual fact it is potentially more important. By publishing articles on LinkedIn, you are able to share them with your connections and those that follow you. Engagement rates on LinkedIn are actually higher than any other platform due to the professional nature of those using it.

Publishing an article will appear on your connections feed as soon as they have been posted. Another major plus with LinkedIn, is that even if you are not connected with someone, they are able to follow you through your article. So the next one you post will appear on their feed also. Articles that you post can turn into lead generation.

Post Daily Updates

LinkedIn operates very similar to all other social media platforms. You need to make sure you are posting on a daily basis. This will give you the best chance to engage, and interact with your connections. You do not need to post a unique update each day, or unique piece of content. You should employ the following:

- Reshare content that someone else has posted
- Link your website so people have a destination for your details
- Repurpose the content in which you have posted on your other social media.

Join Groups

LinkedIn has a unique option where you are able to join groups which are associated with your field of expertise. Here you will find people working in your industry, or those who are looking for information on what you do. This can present the perfect time to discuss your expertise, and also sell your services.

Be aware, using LinkedIn to sell is not the best way to utilize the platform. Those who see sales posts tend to scroll past. However, be informative and demonstrate your knowledge. This will help you to generate leads.
Just try (and retry) these PPJ hack repeatedly for 4 weeks and see what the quality of leads you would generate for your own business or company.

Try LinkedIn Premium

If you use LinkedIn to find, connect and build relationships with your leads or prospects, you may find that the free version of LinkedIn limits your efforts.

But is LinkedIn Premium worth the investment?

In the subsection of this companion handbook, I have revealed the benefits of LinkedIn Premium for you. Jump straight into it!

Benefits of LinkedIn Premium

Here is a list of tools and features you can access with your LinkedIn Premium Business subscription to help you decide whether it is right for you:

1. Extended LinkedIn Network Access

Perhaps the most useful feature you get with LinkedIn Premium is the *Extended LinkedIn Network Access*, which removes the search limitations of the *Commercial Use Limits* of the free accounts.

If you use LinkedIn's Advanced Search to find and connect with prospects, the Commercial Use Limits can greatly hinder your efforts. With the Premium membership, you will not lose access to search results part way through the month, which will negatively affect your lead generation capabilities.

Activities LinkedIn counts towards the Commercial Use Limits include:

- searching for LinkedIn profiles on LinkedIn.com and the mobile app
- browsing LinkedIn profiles using the People Also Viewed section located on the right rail of a profile.

Activities that do not count toward the limit include:

- searching profiles by name using the search box located at the top of every page on LinkedIn.com
- browsing your 1st-degree connections from the Connections page
- searching for jobs on the Jobs page

2. InMail

It interests me to repeat the use of InMail messages here because I know the extent of its contribution to closing and retaining quality leads when used effectively. If you want to send a message directly to someone you are not connected to (and with whom you do not share a group), you must send them an *InMail*.

InMail messages can be useful when you want to message a prospect before you send them a connection request or when they have not accepted your connection request. Sending an InMail, particularly to an in-demand decision-maker, is a great way to establish an initial connection, without that person feeling they are obligated to accept an invitation to connect with someone they do not know.

Additionally, InMail gives you more room to write your message as connection requests can have only 300 characters while an InMail message can have up to 200 characters in the subject line and up to 1900 characters in the body of the message. This can make it easier for you to explain why you are reaching out.

InMail is possible only with a paid membership subscription (Premium or Sales Navigator). Based on your subscription level, you are given a certain number of InMail messages to send every month with an opportunity to purchase more. You get 15 InMail messages a month with the Premium Business membership.

3. Who's Viewed My Profile

You can find an excellent source of new leads in the *Who's Viewed My Profile* section.

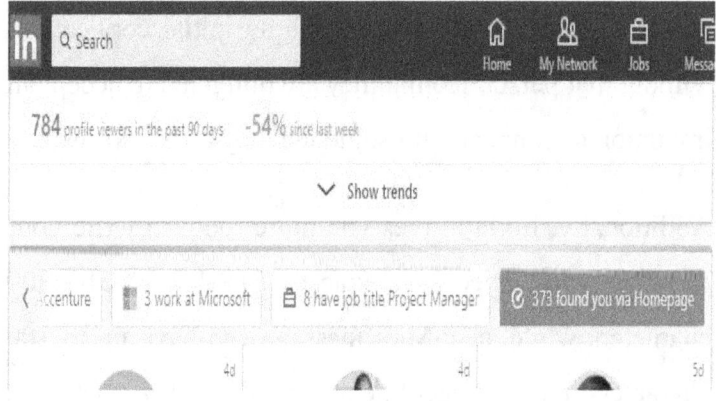

This section lists all the people who have viewed your profile over the last 90 days (you can see only the last five people with a free account).

At the top of the page, you will see a graph showing you how many people are viewing your profile each week. This can help you spot increases or decreases of traffic to your account. When you see an increase, figure out what activities you did that week that could have caused the increase, and then do that activity more regularly to increase the number of people viewing your profile.

LinkedIn also provides you with a couple of basic filters below the top graph, showing you the companies, the people were from, the most common job titles of the viewers, and how they found your profile.

Review the people who have viewed your profile for leads and prospects. For example, let us say some of my ideal clients are corporate trainers. LinkedIn data shows some of them have visited my profile. Using that information, I can quickly and easily compile a list of prospects who already know a little bit about me as I know they have viewed my profile.

When you reach out to these people, do not say "I saw you viewed my profile" or go directly into a sales pitch for your products or services. Instead, review their profiles and look for commonalities. Then send them a thoughtful personalized connection request.

4. Open Profile & Gold Badge

Open Profile is a great feature of LinkedIn Premium as it gives you the option to allow people outside your network to send you a message.

This can be a significant benefit to you as a Premium subscriber if you are using LinkedIn for lead generation. InMails can be costly, and in most cases, prospects will not pay to message you. *Open Profile* removes a key barrier between you and the prospects outside your 1st level network.

When you have the Open Profile feature, LinkedIn members not connected to you will see they can send you a message in the top portion of the profile, even though you are not 1st-degree connections.

Plus, your LinkedIn profile looks more eye-catching in the search results because it has a small gold LinkedIn badge beside your name.

Seemingly a very small benefit, this feature, identifying you as a LinkedIn Premium user, makes you stand out in the search results. This badge can also increase trust and improve your credibility in the eyes of the people you are trying to connect with as most fake accounts and spammers are not paying for the Premium membership.

5. LinkedIn Learning
Another little-known benefit of LinkedIn Premium is the access it gives you to over 13,000 courses created by industry experts on LinkedIn Learning and Lynda.com.

LinkedIn collects and analyzes the skills and jobs data to identify emerging training trends and needs. It then uses that data to create new high-quality courses to keep its library fresh with dozens of courses added every week.

You will find courses in the business, technology, and creative categories. Business courses will help you sharpen your leadership, communication, digital transformation skills, and the likes. Technology courses will help you build your expertise in modern programming languages and computing platforms. And creative courses from Lynda.com will teach you how to bring your ideas to life.

Is LinkedIn Premium worth the investment?

If you are not sure whether you would benefit from upgrading to the Premium membership, you can start with a free 30-day trial so you can test the features.

How much does LinkedIn Premium cost?

After your free month, you will pay per month when billed monthly, and per year when billed annually. (Amounts vary based on currency and country.)

If you use LinkedIn for lead generation, Sales Navigator is a far wiser investment than LinkedIn Premium. For an additional monthly cost, the exceptional number of additional features and benefits Sales Navigator offers makes it a clear winner for the serious social seller.

But do not take this handbook as a promotion for LinkedIn Premium or Sales Navigator. My advice is unbiased as I have no affiliation with LinkedIn, nor do I receive any financial compensation from it.

If you do not think the features mentioned in this book will be useful to you, a free LinkedIn account may be all you need. I still highly recommend the free account to many growing individual business owners and friends if it is clear they will not take any advantage of the additional benefits of LinkedIn Premium.

On the other hand, if you are responsible for business development, lead generation, or sales, I would advise you to consider signing up for Sales Navigator. It far exceeds the benefits of LinkedIn Premium when it comes to aiding you in your lead generation efforts, giving you access to the Sales Navigator features.

CONCLUSION

LinkedIn Sales Navigator can be a powerful tool to improve your lead generation and sales strategies, but it cannot be the only tool you use. Good lead generation strategies rely on a variety of different channels and sources of traffic, and at the end of the day, you will still rely on conventional communication media like email and phone calls—which you will need to track and analyze if you want to succeed.

LinkedIn is one of the best platforms for generating leads. Having a presence on this platform allows your business to be noticed by others, allows you to interact with others, as well as gain valuable knowledge from key decision makers. Navigating the minefield which is LinkedIn can sometimes be difficult, and understanding that there are some interesting characters is part of the fun. Give it a go!

www.ingramcontent.com/pod-product-compliance
Lightning Source LLC
Chambersburg PA
CBHW050308220526
45465CB00002B/873